EXPLORE...

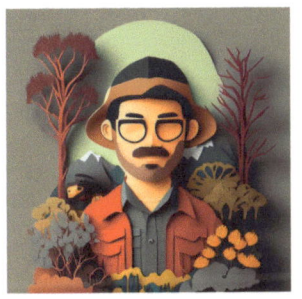

In 20 years, you'll be more disappointed in the things you didn't do than you did.
Then let it go. Let the trade winds fill your sails. Explore. Dream.

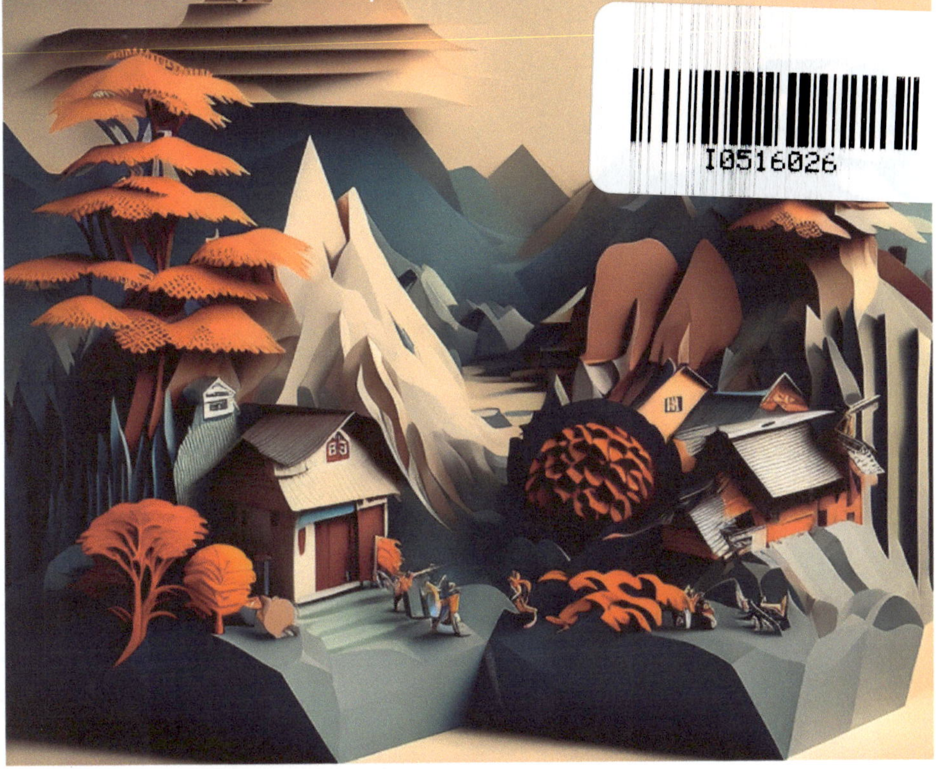

I0516026

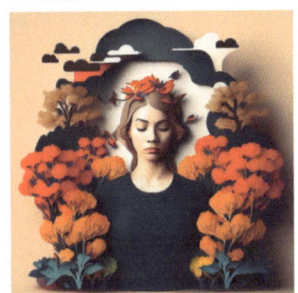

...DREAM!

MY EXPECTATIONS

MY TRIP

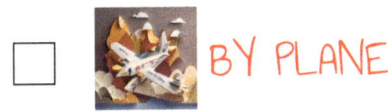

☐ **BY PLANE**

Flag the veichle you used or stick your ticket!

FLIGHT INFORMATION
AIRLINE:

FLIGHT NUMBER:

DEPARTURE TIME:

ARRIVAL TIME:

FLIGHT INFORMATION
AIRLINE:

FLIGHT NUMBER:

DEPARTURE TIME:

ARRIVAL TIME:

FLIGHT INFORMATION
AIRLINE:

FLIGHT NUMBER:

DEPARTURE TIME:

ARRIVAL TIME:

FLIGHT INFORMATION
AIRLINE:

FLIGHT NUMBER:

DEPARTURE TIME:

ARRIVAL TIME:

☐ **BY TRAIN**

☐ **BY BUS**

☐ **BY CAR**

NOTES:

ARC DE TRIOMPHE
Paris Triumphal Arch stands tall

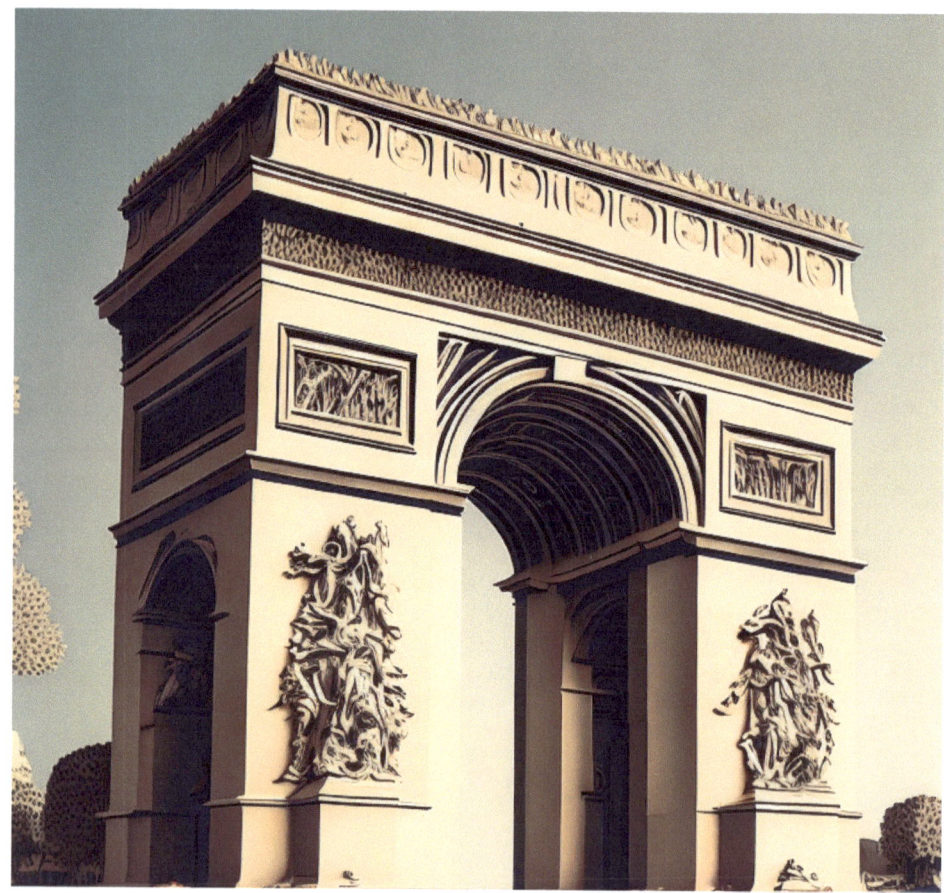

The iconic Arc de Triomphe in Paris, France, stands as a magnificent symbol of triumph and French history. Completed in 1836, it honors those who fought and died during the French Revolution and Napoleonic Wars. Its grandeur, intricate sculptures, and panoramic views make it a must-visit landmark, embodying the city's enduring spirit.

MY MEMORY PICTURE

Stick your photo here!

WHO WAS WITH ME?
_____
_____
_____

WHAT DID I EAT?
_____
_____
_____

NOTES: _____

DATE _____

CATHEDRALE NOTRE-DAME

Gothic masterpiece

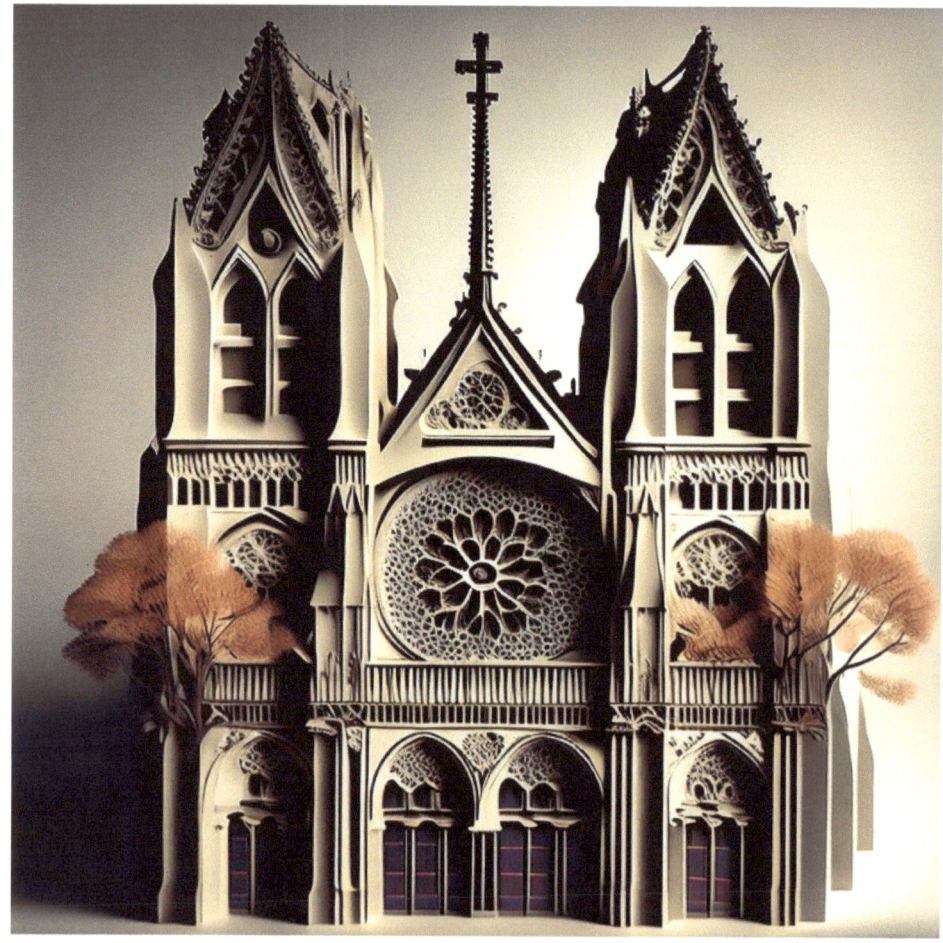

Notre Dame Cathedral in Paris is a magnificent Gothic masterpiece, known for its stunning architecture and historical significance. Built between the 12th and 14th centuries, it has witnessed countless events, including coronations and famous literary inspirations. Its exquisite stained glass windows and iconic gargoyles captivate visitors, making it a cherished symbol of French heritage. Though damaged by fire in 2019, restoration efforts ensure its enduring legacy.

MY MEMORY PICTURE

Stick your photo here!

WHO WAS WITH ME?

WHAT DID I EAT?

🌿 NOTES: _____

DATE _____

MUSEE DU LOUVRE
Art's grand sanctuary

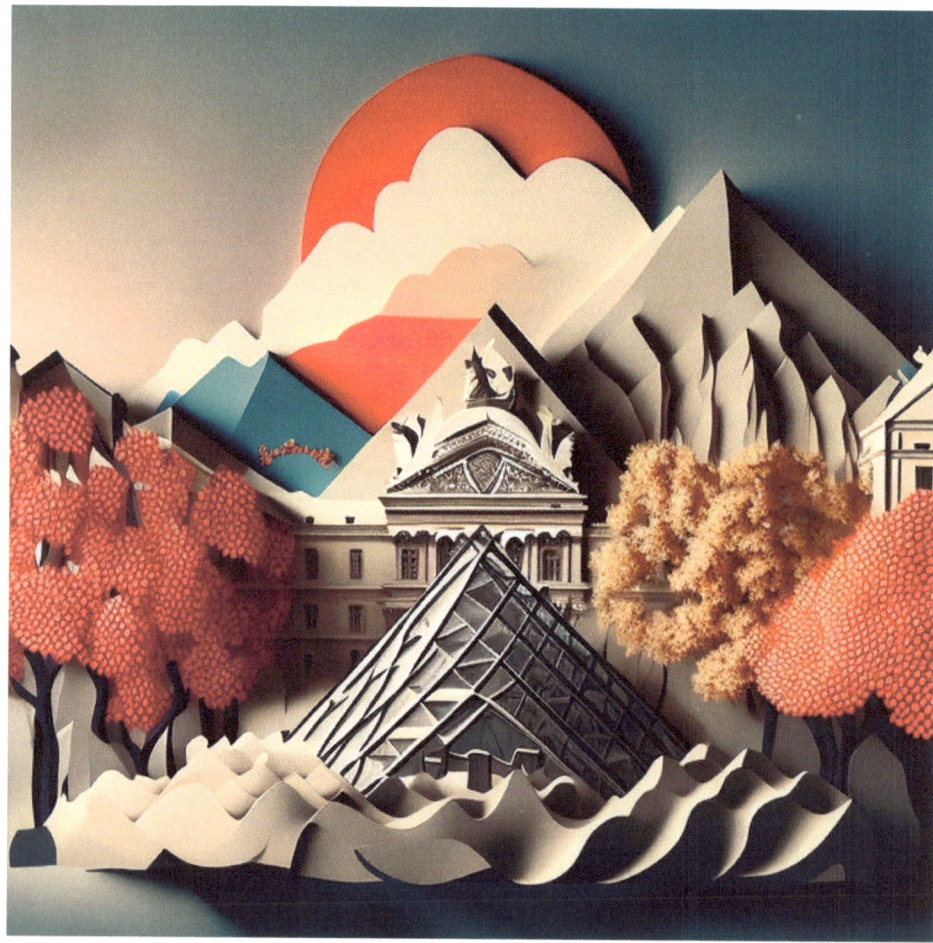

The Louvre Museum in Paris is a treasure trove of art and history. Originally a medieval fortress, it transformed into a grand palace in the 16th century and later became a museum in 1793. With over 38,000 artworks, including the iconic Mona Lisa, it showcases ancient civilizations, Renaissance masterpieces, and global cultural heritage. Its architectural splendor and extensive collections make it a mecca for art enthusiasts worldwide.

MY MEMORY PICTURE

Stick your photo here!

WHO WAS WITH ME?

WHAT DID I EAT?

NOTES:

DATE

TOUR EIFFEL

Parisian landmark icon

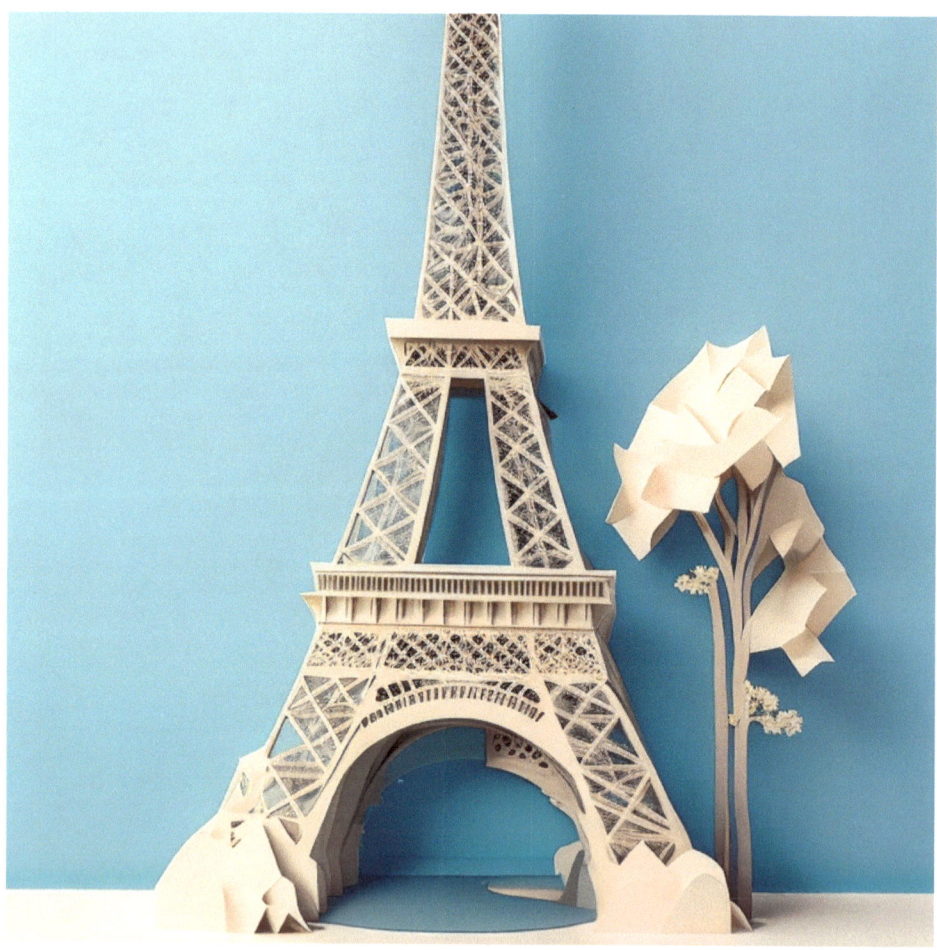

The Eiffel Tower, an architectural marvel in Paris, stands as a symbol of elegance and engineering prowess. Completed in 1889 as the entrance to the World's Fair, it initially faced criticism but soon captured hearts. Today, its iron lattice design and panoramic views attract millions, offering a timeless experience that embodies the city's charm and innovation.

MY MEMORY PICTURE

Stick your photo here!

WHO WAS WITH ME?

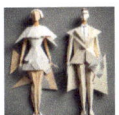
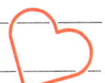

WHAT DID I EAT?

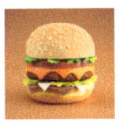

NOTES: _____

DATE _____

PALAIS DE VERSAILLES

Opulent royal grandeur

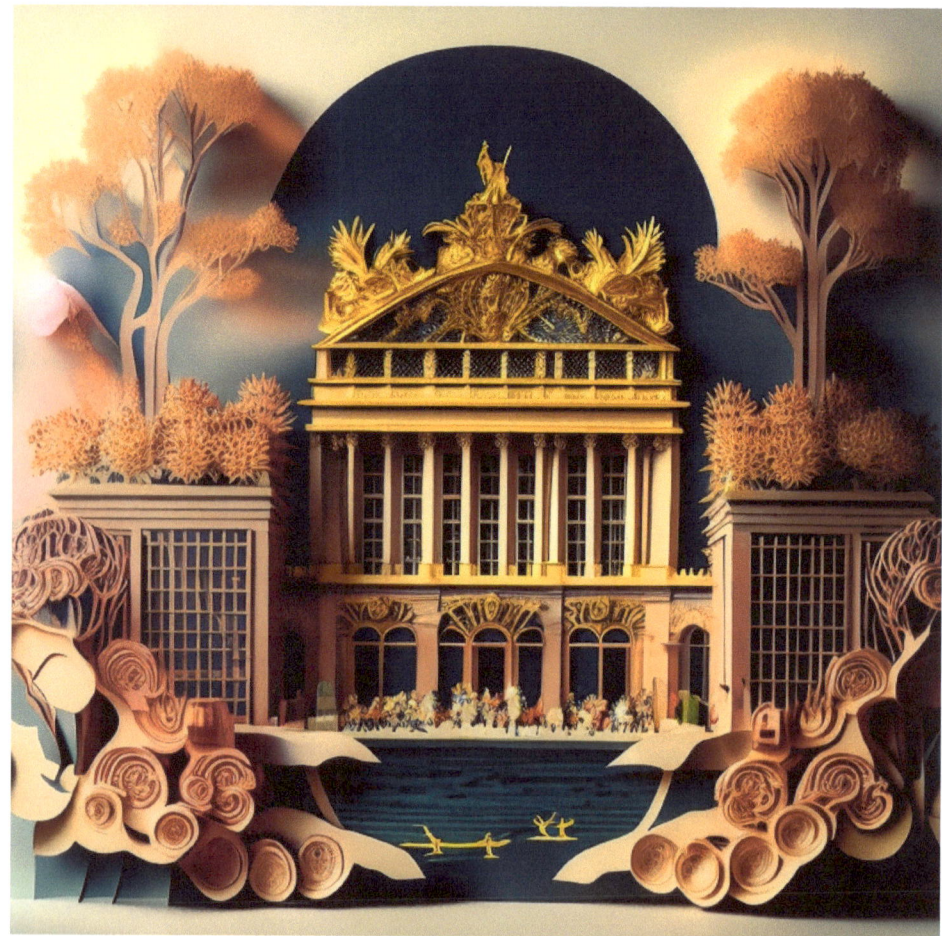

The opulent Palace of Versailles in Paris is a testament to the grandeur of French royalty. Built in the 17th century, it served as the principal residence of Louis XIV and subsequent monarchs. Its magnificent architecture, lavish gardens, and exquisite interior decorations reflect the power and wealth of the French monarchy. Today, it stands as a UNESCO World Heritage site, attracting visitors with its rich history and artistic splendor.

MY MEMORY PICTURE

Stick your photo here!

WHO WAS WITH ME?

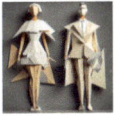

WHAT DID I EAT?

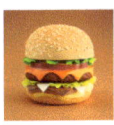

NOTES: _____

DATE _____

MUSEE D'ORSAY

Artistic treasure reborn

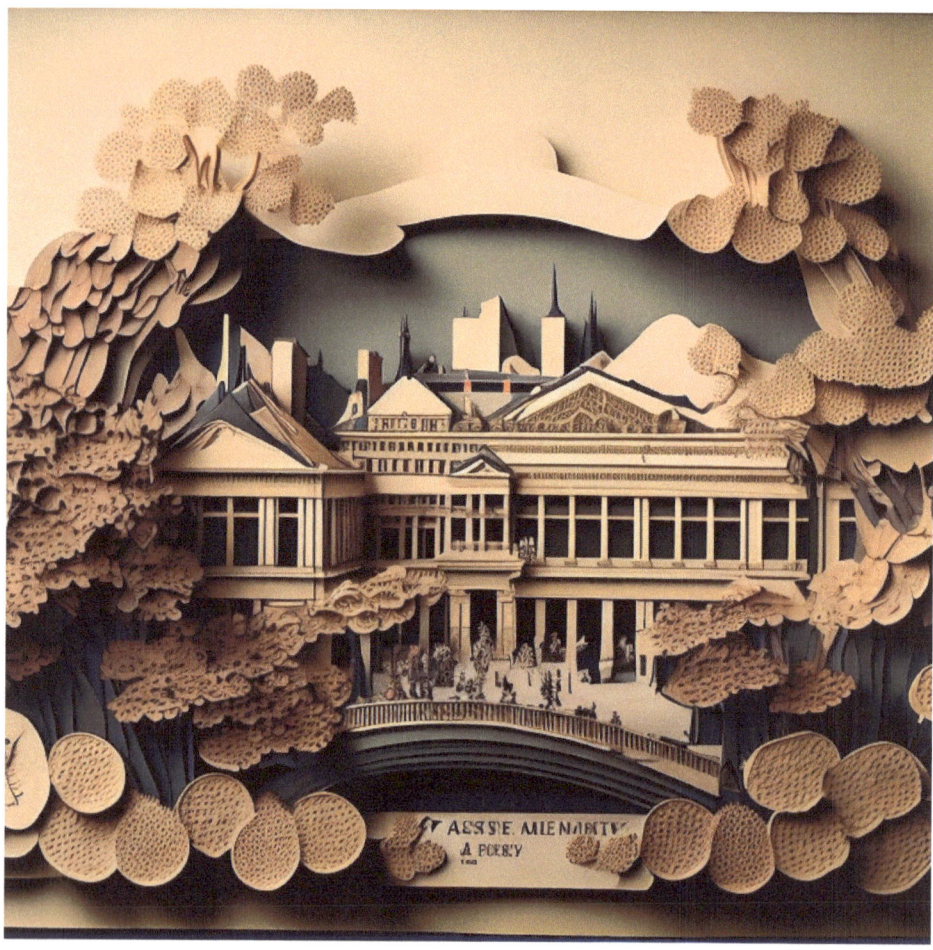

The Musée d'Orsay in Paris is a cultural gem housed in a former railway station. It showcases an extensive collection of Impressionist and Post-Impressionist art, including masterpieces by Monet, Van Gogh, and Renoir. The museum's stunning architecture, blending the old and the new, provides a unique backdrop for appreciating these artistic treasures. With its rich history and remarkable artworks, the Musée d'Orsay captivates art enthusiasts from around the world.

MY MEMORY PICTURE

Stick your photo here!

WHO WAS WITH ME?

WHAT DID I EAT?

NOTES:

DATE

BASILIQUE DU SACRE'-COEUR

Spiritual sanctuary atop

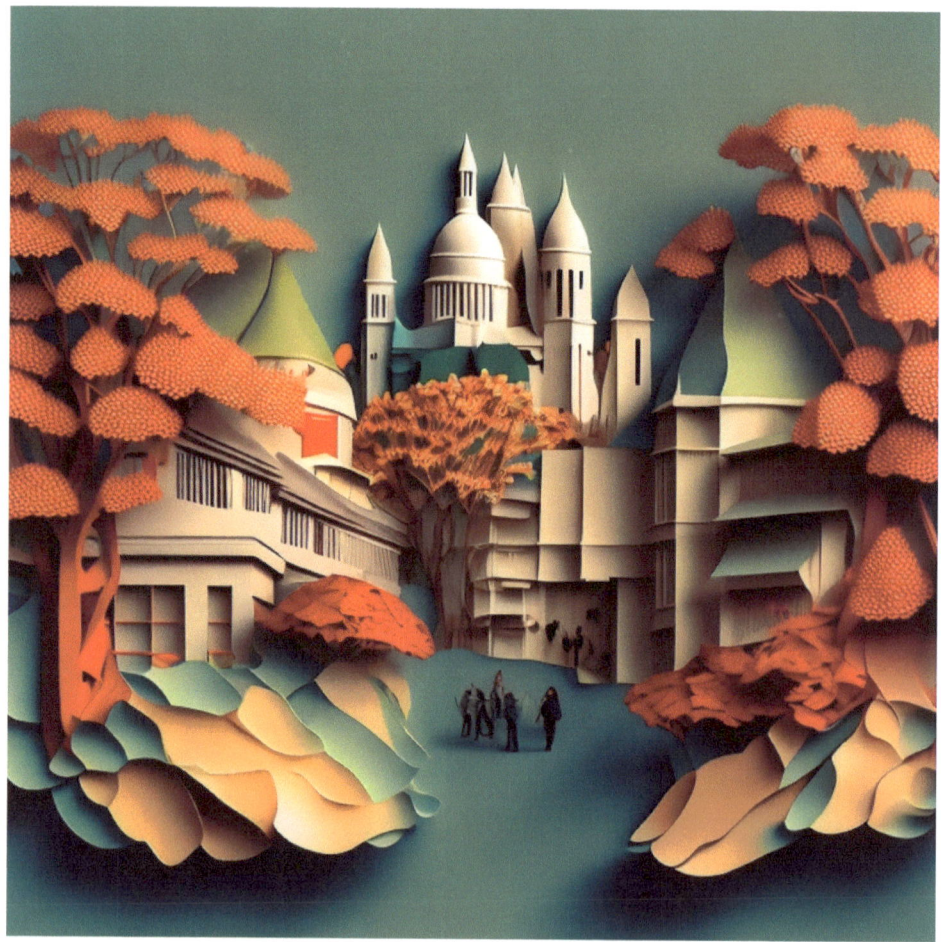

The Sacré-Cœur Basilica in Paris is a majestic spiritual sanctuary situated atop Montmartre hill. Constructed in the late 19th century as a symbol of hope and healing after the turmoil of the Franco-Prussian War, it boasts a distinctive white façade and offers panoramic views of the city. Its serene interior, adorned with beautiful mosaics, invites visitors to find solace and reflect. The Sacré-Cœur Basilica stands as an iconic landmark and a testament to faith in the heart of Paris.

MY MEMORY PICTURE

Stick your photo here!

WHO WAS WITH ME?

WHAT DID I EAT?

NOTES:

DATE

OPERA GARNIER

National opera of Paris

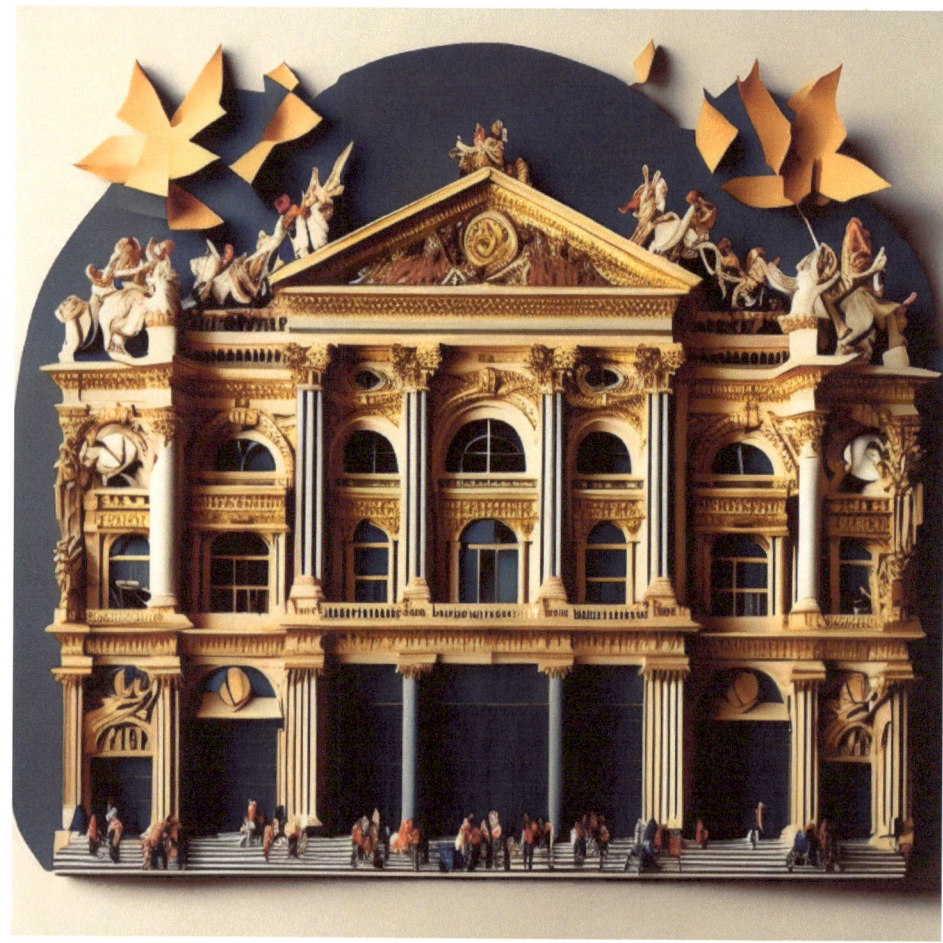

The Opéra Garnier in Paris is a mesmerizing architectural masterpiece and a symbol of grandeur. Designed by Charles Garnier and inaugurated in 1875, it showcases opulent interiors, including the grand staircase and the ornate auditorium. This historic opera house has hosted countless performances, captivating audiences with its exquisite performances and preserving a rich legacy of music and culture. Today, it remains an iconic landmark and a testament to Parisian artistic heritage.

MY MEMORY PICTURE

Stick your photo here!

WHO WAS WITH ME?

WHAT DID I EAT?

NOTES:

DATE

SAINTE-CHAPELLE

Divine beauty in Paris

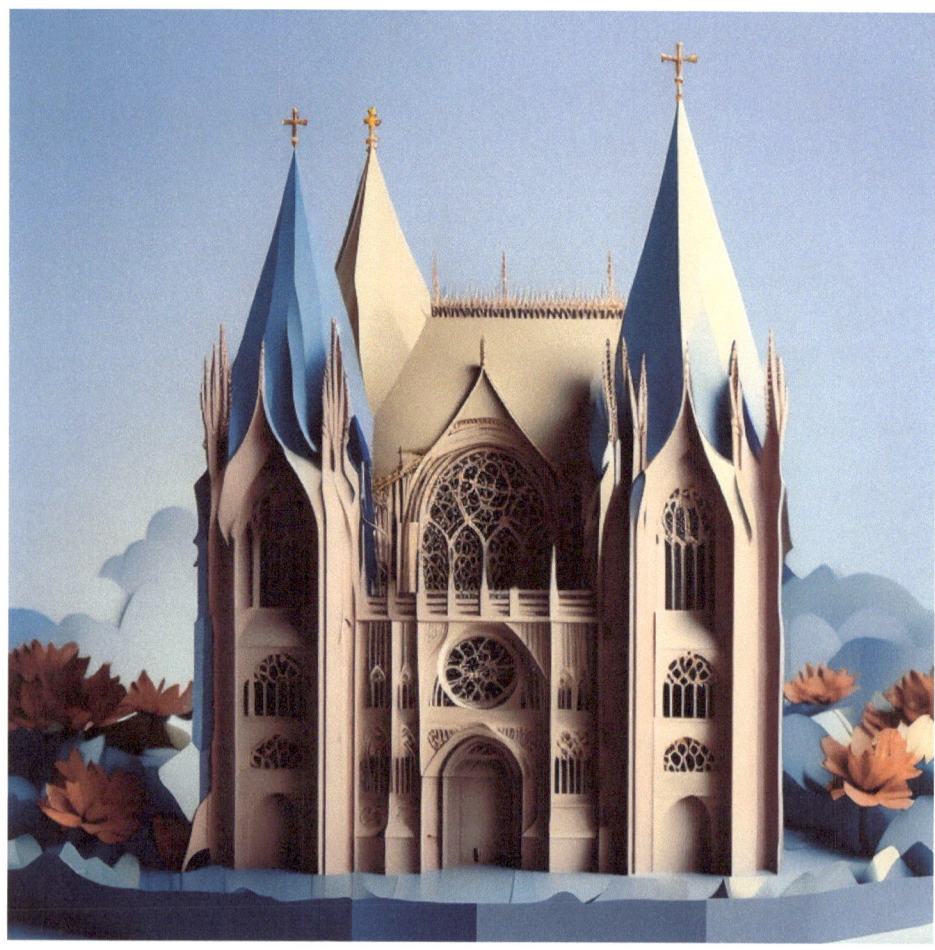

The Sainte-Chapelle in Paris is a stunning example of Gothic architecture and a treasure trove of stained glass artistry. Built in the 13th century by Louis IX, it was intended to house important relics, including the Crown of Thorns. Its towering stained glass windows depict biblical scenes, immersing visitors in a kaleidoscope of vibrant colors. Today, the Sainte-Chapelle stands as a remarkable testament to medieval craftsmanship and a place of awe-inspiring beauty.

MY MEMORY PICTURE

Stick your photo here!

WHO WAS WITH ME?

WHAT DID I EAT?

NOTES:

DATE

SECRET SPOTS
A list of ten hidden gems in the city

Flag the ones that you were able to find and visit!

- [ ] 1. Le squat du 59 rue de Rivoli
- [ ] 2. Le mur des je t'aime
- [ ] 3. Rue Crèmieux
- [ ] 4. Parc des Buttes-Chaumont
- [ ] 5. Petite Ceinture
- [ ] 6. Sacré-Cœu in Montmartre
- [ ] 7. Statue of liberty, pont de Grenelle
- [ ] 8. The hidden little red car outisde Meric in Le Marais
- [ ] 9. La recyclerie
- [ ] 10. Les catacombes de Paris

MY FAVOURITE:
_____
_____
_____

MY SECRET PLACE!
Something that I won't forget...

Stick your photo here!

WHO WAS WITH ME?

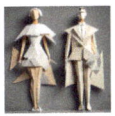

WHAT DID I EAT?

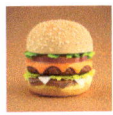

NOTES: _____

DATE _____

NOTES

NOTES

www.ingramcontent.com/pod-product-compliance
Lightning Source LLC
Chambersburg PA
CBHW040308220526
45473CB00002B/604